anatomy

i wrote

from my knees

praying

for the strength

to rise

these words

found me

held me

healed me

thank you

for reading my heart

with yours

we lust

we love

we fall

we rise

our bodies

they feel it all

hips [11]

heart [33]

knees [55]

spine [85]

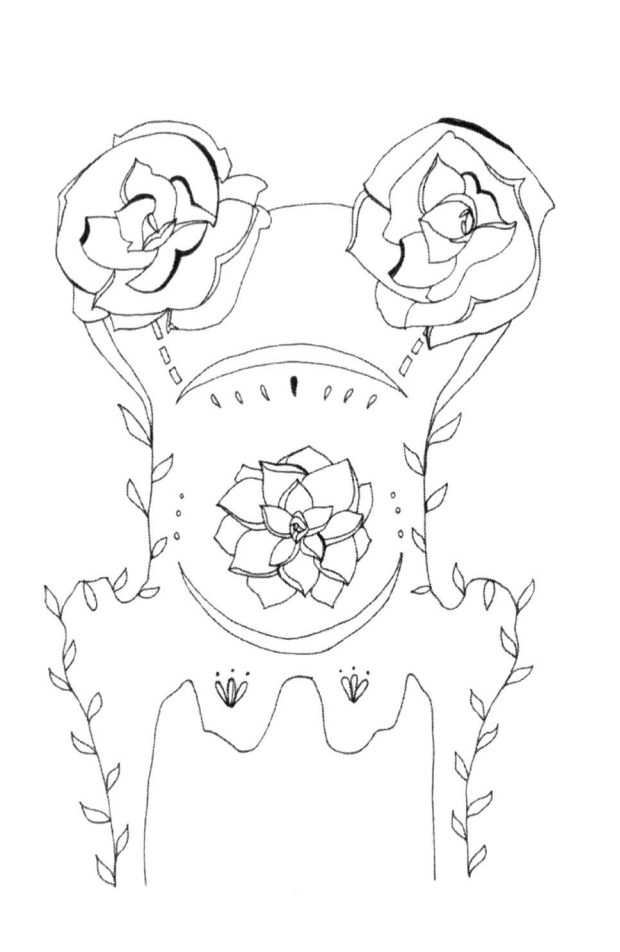

hips
[we lust]

to the men

who lusted

recklessly after me

grasping desperately at my body

tearing off chunks of my soul

with every poetic rejection

every conscious excuse

sweeping past my heart

because they didn't need another

they had one

waiting

at home

to these men

i say

thank you

for bringing me to my knees

these pages are my rising

                                                : teachers

[franks martin]

do not worship me

i don't want you on your knees

i want you side by side

with the moon

the stars

and i

                                    : goddess

look me in the eyes and tell me

you're not terrified

of how i make you feel

i don't play with fire

i am the fire

feel me light you up

listen.

that silence

is our bodies talking

when our mouths don't know how

					: unspoken

[franks martin]

come here

with those beautifully

destructive

electric

hands

hips

lips

i don't know where they've been

but i guess

that's half the fun

[franks martin]

you say

we are connected

i say

do you say the same to her?

                                                           : i know

my victim was wondering

can your narcissist come out to play?

i've got some stories to create

and a heart to break

[franks martin]

next time

please let my lesson

taste less like your lips

feel less like your skin

move less like your hips

next time

please leave a piece of me

left to learn

: anatomy

is this a dance or is this a deathmatch?

: lust

it could have been

delicious

raw

passionate

love

if it weren't for those sunset eyes

                              : abandon ship

you think you know me

but you have no idea

you have only brushed my surface

with your lips

grazed my depths

with your fingertips

: unfinished

[franks martin]

i'll show you

just how sweet

i can be

when you're begging for a taste

and i loosen up the buttons

on my sugar coat

drown you in

my honey

make you

wish you

never

called me that

                                                : sweetie

i want a goddess

he says

really

i say

which one?

: kali

tell me

does it soothe you

when we're on your sofa

not in her bed

: ?

talk dirty to me:

tell me

you love me

[franks martin]

i have never wanted to hold someone

so closely

so intensely

so tightly

yet

known that beauty is born

in the space

between us

[franks martin]

do you realise

you crave me

your body

gives you away

your eyes

betray you

your lips

deceive you

[franks martin]

heal me

with those hands

of yours

my hips are begging

for your touch

my heart is screaming

she knows

what's next

[franks martin]

heart

[we love]

i will raise hell

with an open heart

and banshee lungs

howling my truth

until it is acceptable

to feel

[franks martin]

i laugh

at your jokes

you crack me up

i say

if only you knew

how true that is

my whole heart wants to dive

out of these fractures in my chest

envelope you

thank you

most of all

love you

[franks martin]

we cannot possibly

comprehend

how infinite

we are

stay wildly curious

about your depths

edges

power

heart

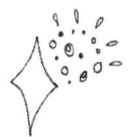

i'm sat by the waves

breathing salty air

counting my blessings

i skip over you

a few times

brow creased

no

i won't

i can't

count him

then i recall

who reminded me to blow a lifetime of dust

from the strength i use

for boundaries

i smile

laugh

and count you five times over

[franks martin]

i wonder

what would happen

if we treated every heart

as if it were our own?

here's to the open hearted

whose edges are shaped

from loving hard

and trusting harder

[franks martin]

the way you hold me

without touching me

takes my breath away

[franks martin]

this one

is for the men

standing strong

holding space

holding hearts

holding us;

while we write fire

for those who burnt us

                                        : brave heart

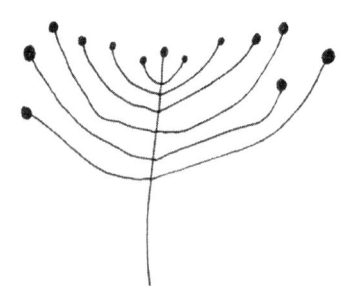

[franks martin]

he whispers

she

is a woman of extremes

she

offers up her whole heart

or nothing at all

[franks martin]

someone once told me

to hold back

once in a while

reign it in

just a little

they said

these words

they are lost on me

half-way

half-hearted

half-in

are not ways i wish to live

i will risk the deepest lows

for the view from the top

we are given whole hearts

for a reason

[franks martin]

inspiration

means

feels

looks

sounds

to me

like you

: muse

you are the first one

i hear my heart call out for

it is usually

these screaming hips

that drown everything out

[franks martin]

at last

a man that can hold

more than just my body

                                         : space

[franks martin]

i wish

that more women

demanded your heart

not your feathers

when you are open

you are divine

                                                  : peacock

take my hand

let's dive over the edge

of this pedestal

and fall in dirty

normal

love

                                                        : ground

[franks martin]

deeply

fully

unapologetically

are the only ways i love

i do not care

what you look like

under that happy shiny

mask

let your truth spill over

your edges

let your flaws surge through

your scars

let your shadows

your tears

your pain

engulf you

i'll be here

rock steady

heart open

loving you

through it all

                                            : self love

[franks martin]

ask your heart what it wants

create stillness

peace

space

then listen

feel

breathe

now choose

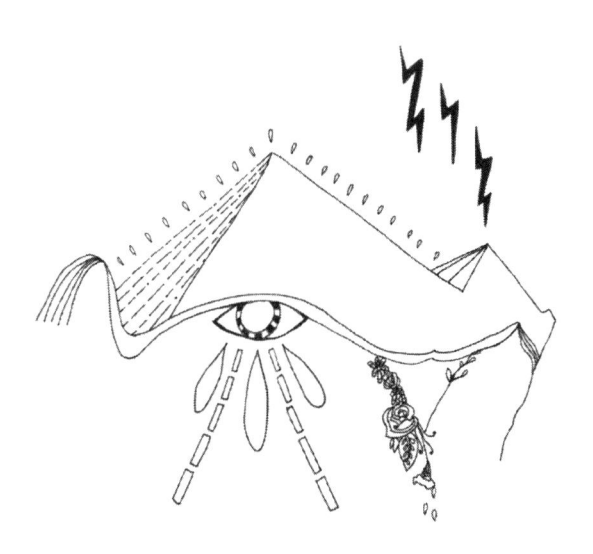

knees

[we fall]

bring me to my knees

i dare you

we like to romanticise

the destruction of hearts

the becoming

of expression

the fuel

for creation

but know this:

there are not always words

poems

lyrics

paintings

sometimes

the art is in

the healing

the learning

to love

again

[franks martin]

you knew my shadows so well

when my light crept in

you left

[franks martin]

'heartbreak'

as if

it's only the space

in our chest

that shatters

tell this to my hips

that grind

to a halt

my jaw

that clenches

tight

my shoulders

that cave

over

my stomach that writhes

in knots

tell them

it's just our hearts that break

[franks martin]

i wonder if you know

how deeply

you tore open

these wounds

i asked you to heal

you said

you were excited

to be around

when i stepped into my power

well here i am

and you

are nowhere to be seen

[franks martin]

inhale

expand

your lies

pause

exhale

contract

your heart

that's not how they teach it

but i guess

that's how you like it

                                                : breathwork

they don't write the songs

about the friends that got away

the ones who twist you in two

make you forget who

you are

they don't tell you the ways in which to heal

from the friends who masquerade

the ones who question until you

question who

you are

they don't tell you how to cut loose

the friends who dance across your buttons

the ones who know too much

make you hate who

you are

[franks martin]

today

i fill up my cup

with tears

tomorrow

it will be

might be

love

[franks martin]

do not judge me

based on the parts of me

your body does not allow you to receive

i am not here to fill you up

                                            : leave

[franks martin]

and then some days

there are no words

breathing

is enough

[franks martin]

the trouble starts

when you step into my light

bask

bathe

let it fill you

to the brim

glowing

from my radiance

and suddenly

i'm left

with embers

[franks martin]

someday

we will realise

people don't break hearts

expectations do

you are a breath of fresh air

you tell me

but i know

you're lying

we need air

to live

you do not need me

she is your air

i am your sunshine

on a summer's day

glorious

light

expansive

beaming

but fleeting

delicious

to experience

but you can live

without it

[franks martin]

how do we fall

so easily

for our mirrors

yet

struggle to care

for ourselves?

[franks martin]

i'm not sure

                                                  there's someone else

you're too much

                    : three words / i've been waiting for

[franks martin]

be careful

with those walls

you build so well

some day

we will all grow tired

from climbing

[franks martin]

my head

is at home in confusion

my heart

does not belong here

tell me

how you feel

[franks martin]

and

when i am face down

worn

from the empty hearts

i've been trying to fill

the earth will greet me

embrace me

whispering

"stay open

love on

anyway"

[franks martin]

you said i was the light

is that why

you were moth

to my flame

hypnotised

by me

leaving

on to the next

when i burnt out

[franks martin]

i dance over

your walls

with ease

at first

my fleeting footsteps

sidestep your fences

with a wink

and a smile

but the walls

they become castles

castles become towers

kissing the clouds

and i am left

heart on my sleeve

peering into your windows

too exhausted to climb

[franks martin]

heartbreak

sounds clean

fast

simple

they should call it

heart splinter

instead

wrap

your fingertips

around my heart strings

pull

a little harder

watch me come undone

[franks martin]

mornings

are the worst

my heart is so heavy

it pins me down

i am suffocating

hostage to my sheets

[franks martin]

it's the shame

that burns

it was never you

you are not the thing

that breaks me

[franks martin]

how do you grieve

for someone

that was never truly

here?

[franks martin]

spine
[we rise]

one day

you will feel me rise

so explosively

expansively

there will be nothing left of you

but rubble

one day

soon

                                                    : watch

people tell you they know heartbreak

as if we each crack open

the same way

as if we each rise up on

the same route

as if we each heal

the same wounds

this is my invitation to you:

know that you are alone

on this journey

through your body

no one else

can own this pain

but we are all here

falling

to our knees

stumbling

with abandoned hips

[franks martin]

growing

whole-heartedly

resurrecting

backbones

rising

beside you

[franks martin]

i am learning

that the ones who got away

are often

the ones who ran away

: let them go

do not try to fix me

hold me

while i fix myself

[franks martin]

don't be surprised

that someone else is picking up

my pieces

kissing them gently

replacing them softly

patiently waiting

for me to come home

to myself

: healing

you were right

i took that bite

out of life

watch it trickle down my chin

drip into my heart

fill me up

in the places that you couldn't

: lioness

we both know

you catch women

like you catch those waves

confidently

smoothly

often

just remember

                              these women

                                those waves

                                    and i

                        we are forces of nature

                              you may ride

                                for a while

                                but in the end

                        we will consume you

                              devastate you

                                  leave you

                              gasping for air

                    and you will understand

[franks martin]

we will not

can not

be controlled

[franks martin]

you can replace me

but you will never

ever

forget me

remember when

you took my voice

all of those years

lies

and women

ago

i found it

[franks martin]

we are crawling

but we are still moving forward

[franks martin]

i am

as deep

as i am light

i am not for the weak of heart

honour this

or step aside

[franks martin]

i have never heard

the ocean

apologise

for its depth

do not be sorry

for yours

[franks martin]

we are not born

resilient

something happens when

our wounds

heal over we

move a little steadier

flow a little smoother

dip a little deeper

dance a little harder

rise

a little faster

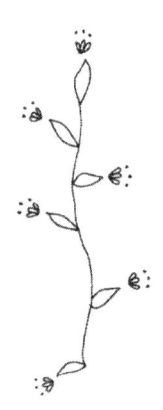

: strength

i prefer empathy

to sympathy

but my goodness

you missed out

                                                                         : on me

i am not here

to tiptoe

and whisper

sweet nothings

                              i am here to create

                                        thunder

                                with my lungs

                                          waves

                                with my body

                                           fire

                               with my words

                                     lightning

                               with my heart

i will not be silenced

for your comfort

i was not put on this earth

to impress you

i am here

to be heard

[franks martin]

you would get lost

in my depths

anyway

i'm sorry for your loss

they'll say

as my hips ripple past

your jaw hits the floor

and your heart mourns

for mine

                                            : condolences

permission

to be who i am

is the greatest gift i ever gave myself

it is endless

[franks martin]

stay

so exquisitely true

to yourself

that not a single soul

could doubt your unwavering

devotion

to the path that is

uniquely

unquestionably

divinely

yours

[franks martin]

we are more than just bodies

being dragged through life

we are life

creation

in motion

a myriad of miracles

dancing through space

let's act

think

and love

like this

courageous are the deep lovers

with open hearts

and battle scars

[franks martin]

empowerment isn't always beautiful

it's rugged

rough

crooked

but it makes you feel alive

look at those flowers

showing us how to live:

staying true

to their path

nourishing themselves

navigating darkness

gracefully

rising up

without shame

blossoming

fearlessly

[franks martin]

i am in so deep

i can't catch myself

i am falling so madly

so delightfully

so beautifully

so insanely

in love

with myself

                                        : irrevocable

Printed in Great Britain
by Amazon